Who Was
P. T. Barnum?

by Kirsten Anderson

illustrated by Stephen Marchesi

Penguin Workshop

To all the elephants—KA

To my Starburner Associates and
our Carnival of Inventions—SM

PENGUIN WORKSHOP
An Imprint of Penguin Random House LLC, New York

Text copyright © 2019 by Kirsten Anderson. Illustrations copyright © 2019 by Penguin Random House LLC. All rights reserved. Published by Penguin Workshop, an imprint of Penguin Random House LLC, New York. PENGUIN and PENGUIN WORKSHOP are trademarks of Penguin Books Ltd. WHO HQ & Design is a registered trademark of Penguin Random House LLC. Printed in the USA.

Visit us online at www.penguinrandomhouse.com.

Library of Congress Cataloging-in-Publication Data is available upon request.

ISBN 9780448488486 (paperback)   10 9 8 7 6 5 4
ISBN 9781524792220 (library binding)   10 9 8 7 6 5 4 3 2

Contents

Who Was P. T. Barnum?

At last, the big day was here. Phineas Taylor Barnum was about to see the property that made him the wealthiest boy in Bethel, Connecticut.

His grandfather Phineas Taylor often reminded him how lucky he was to be named after him. After all, that was why he had been given Ivy Island, one of the best pieces of land in the state. When Taylor, as everyone called him, was old enough, he would be able to turn it into rich farmland or sell it at a fantastic price. Taylor nodded. He certainly understood how lucky he was.

Everyone knew about Taylor's island. His mother told him to be grateful for it. His father hoped Taylor would help support the family when the island was finally his. He promised he would. Neighbors hoped Taylor would not forget them when he became rich and powerful. He promised he would not.

Taylor dreamed about Ivy Island and the wonders it would bring him, but he had never actually seen it. Then, in 1822, when he was twelve years old, he asked his father for permission to visit Ivy Island. His father agreed that it was time.

Taylor was so excited, he could barely sleep. On the morning of the visit, his mother told him to try to stay calm when he got there and to not make himself sick with excitement. She hoped that when he came back, he would not feel too important to speak to his brother and sisters. Taylor said he would try to be kind to them.

It was difficult to get to Ivy Island. Taylor's father had one of his farmworkers show Taylor the way. The path was swampy. Taylor had to leap over deep puddles and bogs. He trudged through water and mud. He was attacked by hornets.

Finally they made their way across a stream. The worker who had guided Taylor pointed and said, "There's your Ivy Island!"

Taylor stared. It was a patch of bare land. It had only a few trees and thin plants. It was not a wonderful piece of land that would make him rich. It was probably worth nothing.

Then Taylor realized the truth. He had been the victim of one of his fun-loving grandfather's jokes. And it wasn't just him—Taylor's parents, neighbors, and the whole town had been in on it! When he got home, they all laughed at him.

Taylor eventually was able to laugh about it, too. And he learned a lesson that stayed with him for the rest of his life: The more effort you put into a practical joke, the funnier it could be. And the Ivy Island story had entertained a lot of people for a very long time.

Phineas Taylor Barnum grew up to become a great showman who entertained people around the world. He learned at a young age how the best, most convincing stories could hold people's interest. In time, he became the owner of "the Greatest Show on Earth."

CHAPTER 1
Connecticut

Phineas Taylor Barnum was born on July 5, 1810, in Bethel, Connecticut. Everyone called him Taylor. His parents were Philo Barnum and Irena Taylor Barnum. Philo was a tailor. He also owned a tavern, part of a general store, and a farm.

Irena's father, Phineas Taylor, was one of the most important people in town. He owned a great deal of land and was a judge. Taylor adored his cheerful grandfather, whom everyone called "Uncle Phin." Taylor said that his grandfather would "go farther, wait longer, work harder . . . to carry out a practical joke, than for anything else under heaven." Uncle Phin wasn't the only one who loved a joke. Taylor later talked about how the whole town loved playing pranks and tricks and telling tall tales. He said that growing up around these people helped him develop his own sense of fun and humor.

Taylor started school at age six. He was excellent at math and enjoyed writing essays and funny bits of poetry. He hated working on his father's farm. He preferred dreaming up ways to make money. He sold candy, cookies, and drinks in town. By the time he was twelve, he had made enough money to buy his own calf and sheep.

Taylor's father noticed how good Taylor was at earning money and announced that from then on, he could pay for his own clothes. He also let Taylor work in the general store when he wasn't in school, instead of on the farm. And Taylor loved working in the store. He listened to the customers' stories and laughed at their jokes. He watched as they bargained over prices and tried to get the best of each other when making trades.

Philo Barnum died in 1826, leaving sixteen-year-old Taylor alone with his mother, younger brother, and three sisters. They had to sell almost everything they owned to pay off their debts.

Taylor took a job in a store in Grassy Plain, a town a mile away from Bethel. One Saturday a pretty young dressmaker named Charity Hallett came from Bethel to buy a hat. A bad storm struck and Taylor offered to help her get home.

By the time they got to Bethel, he was in love with Charity.

In 1827, Taylor was offered a job in Brooklyn, New York. There he learned all about how to manage a store. Taylor enjoyed New York. He went to plays and shows as often as he could.

But Uncle Phin missed Taylor. He offered to give him part of a building in Bethel to start his own store. Taylor was anxious to get back to Charity, so he returned to Bethel.

Taylor opened a store. He also ran lotteries, selling tickets and giving away prizes. He put a lot of effort into advertising his lotteries and made a great deal of money from them.

Taylor wanted to marry Charity, but his mother disapproved. She thought he could do better than a simple dressmaker from Bethel. But Taylor loved Charity.

In October 1829, Charity went to New York to visit relatives. A month later, Taylor went to New York for business. He met up with Charity, and they were married at her uncle's house.

Taylor's mother was very unhappy and at first refused to acknowledge his marriage and new wife. Finally, after about a month, she gave in and accepted Charity. Taylor and Charity were very happy together.

CHAPTER 2
The 161-Year-Old Woman

In the early 1830s, Taylor opened a second store. He also started a newspaper called *Herald of Freedom*. And he continued to make money selling lottery tickets.

In 1834, Connecticut banned lotteries, and Taylor lost one of his main sources of income. He wanted something more than to run a small-town newspaper. He decided that he, Charity, and their new baby, Caroline, would move to New York City.

Taylor opened a small boardinghouse in New York, with rooms to rent and daily meals, and he also became a partner in a grocery store. In 1835, while working in the store, Taylor heard about an opportunity that would change his life.

A customer told him about an enslaved woman named Joice Heth who performed a live stage show. People said she was 161 years old! She claimed to have been George Washington's nanny.

During her show, Joice told stories about "little George" and sang songs. She was blind and could barely move. She certainly looked very old.

Her manager was tired of touring. He wanted someone else to take over the show. Taylor was fascinated. He sold his half of the store and borrowed money to take Joice on tour for twelve months.

Taylor booked a New York theater for Joice's shows. Then he put ads all over the city. He wrote stories about her and glowing reviews of her show for newspapers. Taylor's efforts paid off. Joice Heth's show earned about $1,500 each week! Taylor then sent her off on a tour of New England. The show was very successful.

Joice Heth died in February 1836. But the show—and the story—wasn't quite over. Taylor had promised a doctor that he could study Joice's body to learn how she had managed to live so long. But after the examination, the doctor announced that Joice could have been only eighty years old at the most. Everyone who had paid to see her show had been fooled.

Taylor said that he was just as surprised as everyone else. He had also believed Joice Heth's story. Later some people said that he had faked documents about Joice's age. Newspapers printed stories about the mystery and argued about whether or not Taylor Barnum knew the truth. Taylor didn't mind—after all, he believed that the only bad publicity was "no publicity."

By this time, Taylor had fallen in love with show business. People all over the United States were thrilled by the traveling shows that brought them plays, dancers, singers, magicians, and animal trainers. Audiences turned out in large numbers to see people who had special talents, who looked strange, or who simply told stories about their lives. Taylor had made Joice Heth's story—and her show—a success. By the late 1830s he was looking for other interesting people and strange artifacts. Taylor was ready to put on a new show.

CHAPTER 3
The American Museum

Taylor spent the next
few years managing
performers. He started out
working for a small circus,
and then created his own
show, Barnum's Grand
Scientific and Musical
Theatre. The program
featured a plate spinner,
a singer and dancer, some
musicians, and a magician.
Taylor booked the theaters,
managed publicity, and
even sold the tickets. If
a performer left a tour

suddenly, Taylor himself would step in for him. He sang and danced, and acted as a magician's assistant. He learned enough magic so that, eventually, he could perform an entire magic act to entertain friends.

The life of a traveling showman was hard, though. Taylor found it difficult to be away from his family. In April 1840, his second daughter, Helen, was born. Taylor went home to New York.

The only work he could find in the city was writing ads for newspapers, but that paid very little. He had almost no money. Then, in 1841, he heard that Scudder's American Museum was selling its entire collection.

Early American museums were rarely dedicated to just a single subject, like art, history, or science. They were usually unique collections of many interesting things. Taylor thought he could take the old, dusty items from Scudder's American Museum and turn them into a successful business.

Taylor borrowed money to buy the collection and took over the museum. He immediately went to work. He had paintings of fantastic animals created on the outside walls of the museum and flags installed on the roof and balconies.

Taylor put lights on top of the building. He put posters all over the city and ads in newspapers, telling about the new museum. He made sure that feature stories about the new exhibits appeared in the newspapers.

Scudder's American Museum

More of a sideshow than a traditional art museum, Scudder's American Museum housed live animals, stuffed animals, a guillotine, wax figures, large paintings of cities around the world, and the first American flag raised when the British left the country in 1783.

Founded by John Scudder in 1809, Scudder's American Museum was originally located at 21 Chatham Street in New York City.

Inside Barnum's American Museum, visitors could look at the menagerie (say: muh-NAJ-uh-ree), a collection of live wild animals. There were lions, tigers, a hippopotamus, a giant bear, a giraffe, an orangutan, and snakes. One of the most popular exhibits was the "Happy Family," a group of animals that were usually natural enemies who had been trained to live together in one cage: rabbits and hawks, cats and rats, eagles and mice.

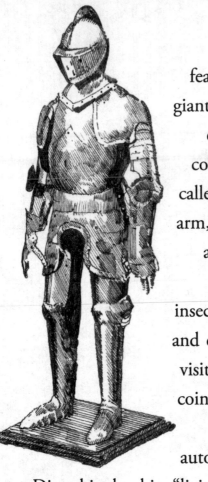

The museum also featured wax figures and giant paintings of famous events. It contained a collection of what were called curiosities: a pirate's arm, a big ball of hair, and a huge magnet. There were exhibits about insects, minerals, seashells, and coral. In other rooms visitors could see ancient coins, suits of armor, trick mirrors, and famous autographs.

Disturbingly, his "living exhibits" featured both animals and people. Some had physical differences that most people had never seen.

There were people with spotted skin, strangely shaped heads, and a bearded lady. The "armless wonder" could play the cello and accordion, and shoot a bow and arrow with his toes.

The Bearded Lady

Visitors to the museum could have their fortunes told. They could buy refreshments and enjoy them on the rooftop deck. They could even have their photographs taken. Photography had only just been invented. In the 1840s, people would never have dreamed of actually owning a camera! Many visitors might have had their photographs first taken at Barnum's American Museum.

Museums were becoming one of the most popular forms of entertainment of the nineteenth century. They had animals and natural history exhibits and historical paintings. They held history and science lectures. Taylor used his museum's lecture room for plays. He put on educational shows that the whole family could enjoy.

Taylor used many tricky ways to sell tickets. He hired a band to play outside the museum, but the musicians were terrible. People would go into the museum just to get away from the awful noise! He sometimes ran contests to attract crowds with cash prizes for best dog, flower, or chicken. The "Finest Baby" contests always drew the most entries.

One of his most famous tricks was putting up signs in the museum that said This Way to the Egress, with an arrow. People followed the signs to see the "egress." But *egress* is just an unusual word for "exit," and the signs led everyone right out of the museum! If the people wanted to get back inside, they had to buy another ticket—and many did.

When visitors to New York City wanted entertainment, they thought of Phineas Taylor Barnum and his sensational museum. Thousands of people visited the museum each year. The American Museum was P. T. Barnum's first big success.

CHAPTER 4
See the Mermaid!

Taylor Barnum never stopped adding to his museum. If he saw something unusual, he tried to buy it. He sent agents around the world to find more odd exhibits and interesting curiosities. He sometimes exchanged items—on loan—with other museums.

In 1842, the owner of the Boston Museum told Taylor that he had bought a mermaid from a sea captain, who had brought it back from India. Taylor immediately made a deal to rent the mermaid from Boston for a few months. Of course it wasn't a real mermaid. A mermaid is a mythical creature described as having the face and body of a beautiful woman and the tail of a fish. The Fejee Mermaid, as it was called, was actually the top half of a stuffed monkey sewn to the tail of a large fish. It was not beautiful. Taylor himself said it was an "ugly, dried-up" thing. He knew it was a fake. But that didn't matter. He believed people would want to see it.

Origin of the Fejee Mermaid

In 1822, an American sea captain named Samuel Edes bought the mermaid from Japanese sailors for $6,000—an enormous amount of money in the 1820s. Edes displayed it in London as the "Fejee Mermaid," named after the island nation in the South Pacific Ocean, whose name is now spelled "Fiji."

After Captain Edes's death, his son sold the mermaid to the Boston Museum in 1842. P. T. Barnum later rented the mermaid from the museum for $12.50 a week.

Today, Harvard University has what may be the original Fejee Mermaid in its Peabody Museum of Archaeology and Ethnology.

In the spring of 1842, New York newspapers began to publish letters from people who were writing in from different parts of the United States. Each of them mentioned "Dr. Griffin," a British scientist who was traveling through America on his way home from a trip to certain islands in the Pacific Ocean. Dr. Griffin said he had collected many interesting things on his trip, including a mermaid.

People in New York became curious about Dr. Griffin and his mermaid. Taylor told the newspapers that he had tried to make a deal with Dr. Griffin to show the mermaid at his museum, but the doctor refused. Taylor said he was terribly upset about this. He even let the newspapers print the ads he had made up with pictures of the mermaid before the

doctor refused to agree to show it. People became even more fascinated by the mermaid.

Of course there was no Dr. Griffin. Taylor had tricked the newspapers into giving him free publicity for the upcoming mermaid exhibit. By the time he announced that Dr. Griffin had changed his mind, New York City had "mermaid fever."

Taylor described the types of tricks he used to get attention for the Fejee Mermaid as "humbugs." Many people in the nineteenth century used the word *humbug* to mean "a fraud" or "a fake." But to Taylor it meant "putting on glittering appearances" or a "show" to get people's attention. He thought humbugs—mild deceptions—were fine as long as people enjoyed what they came to see. He even called himself "the Prince of Humbugs."

In August 1842, after months of creating interest in the story, Taylor finally showed the Fejee Mermaid in his museum. Some people were

The Prince of Humbugs

disappointed when they saw it. The half-monkey, half-fish creature didn't look like the pretty long-haired mermaids on the museum's posters! People argued about whether the mermaid was a fake or not. This was fine with Taylor. The museum's ticket sales tripled.

The Fejee Mermaid was sent on tour throughout the United States in 1843. But the tour ended quickly in South Carolina when a local minister and some scientists called the mermaid a fake. They chased Barnum's employees and the mermaid out of town. The mermaid was eventually put away in a box. Taylor had other things on his mind. He had found his next big star: a talented little boy he called Tom Thumb.

CHAPTER 5
Meet General Tom Thumb

In late 1842, Taylor heard about an unusually small boy named Charley Stratton who lived in Bridgeport, Connecticut. Taylor went to meet him and found a bright-eyed five-year-old who was less than two feet tall! He weighed only sixteen pounds. Doctors thought it was unlikely he would ever grow much more.

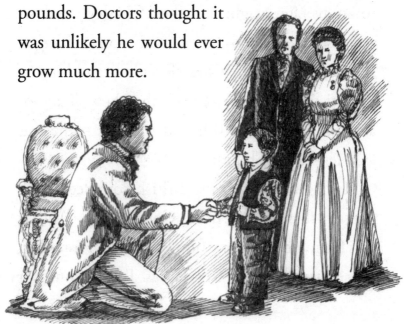

Taylor offered the boy's parents a contract for Charley to perform at the American Museum. Charley and his mother came to New York, and Taylor put together a show for him. Taylor was happy to find that Charley was a quick learner, with a good sense of humor. He loved to tell jokes and make people laugh. Taylor knew audiences would love him.

He worried about Charley's young age, though. People might think he would soon grow to an average height and then Charley wouldn't seem so special. So Taylor made some changes. He said that Charley was eleven years old in the advertisements he wrote for the show. The ads also said he was British and that his name was "General Tom Thumb."

Taylor thought being British sounded much fancier than being from Connecticut. And it was funny to call a tiny boy "General." From then on, everyone knew Charley as Tom Thumb or

simply "the General." The General was an instant
hit at the museum. He performed comedy routines
in different costumes. He sang and danced and

talked to the audience. Children were allowed to come onto the stage to compare their own height to Tom's.

Charley performed at the museum and on tours around the country. But Taylor felt that he was ready for a bigger stage. In January 1844, Taylor, Charley, and his parents left for Europe. Taylor felt terribly homesick as the ship left port.

He would miss Charity and their daughters
Caroline, Helen, and one-year-old baby Frances.
But he knew he could make Charley, performing
as General Tom Thumb, an international star.

Phineas Taylor Barnum and his traveling show arrived in England after eighteen days at sea. He rented a house in a very nice part of London where wealthy and fashionable people lived. He contacted news editors and members of the British nobility and invited them to meet Tom Thumb privately. This stirred up interest in the show and helped Taylor rent a theater where Tom could perform. Soon after the performances began,

Tom Thumb received an invitation to come to Buckingham Palace and meet Queen Victoria!

This was a huge honor. Tom impressed everyone with his fine manners. They all laughed at the skits he performed. Queen Victoria herself gave Tom a tour of the paintings in the palace gallery. Taylor and Tom were invited back several times.

Queen Victoria (1819–1901)

Princess Alexandrina Victoria became the queen of England in 1837 when she was only eighteen years old.

In 1840, Victoria married her cousin Albert. Together she and Prince Albert had nine children and forty-two grandchildren!

By the end of the 1860s, Great Britain had grown as an empire. It ruled many colonies and was a very prosperous nation. Victoria is seen as a symbol of the time when Britain became a great world power.

When Victoria died in 1901, she had been queen for sixty-three years. Her reign is known as the Victorian Era.

The queen's interest in little Tom Thumb made him very popular. Important people wanted to meet Tom. He agreed to private shows and also performed for large theater audiences. Taylor and Tom were both making plenty of money. Taylor even had a tiny carriage built for Tom. Pulled by very small ponies, the carriage was driven around London parks, drawing even more attention.

Everything seemed to be going well, and Tom's popularity was growing. He was earning $500 a day for his performances at a London theater.

His parents earned money from selling souvenirs and pamphlets about their son. But then Taylor received some tragic news. His youngest daughter, Frances, had died. She was less than two years old.

Taylor was deeply saddened. But for the next few years, as Taylor and Tom Thumb toured

Britain and Europe, he made sure that Charity
and his older daughters joined him when they
could. In 1847, the General Tom Thumb show
returned to North America for shows around the
United States, Canada, and Cuba.

Taylor decided to stop managing the Tom Thumb show a year later. He was ready to return home to Charity, Caroline, Helen, and their new baby, Pauline, in New York. The tour had been a huge success. By the time they parted, General Tom Thumb had become a star and P. T. Barnum was a famous showman. Their names were known all over the United States and Europe. They had earned a lot of money together as well. Taylor and Charley remained friends for life.

CHAPTER 6
Introducing Jenny Lind

In 1848, Taylor and his family moved into a new mansion he had had built near Bridgeport, Connecticut. Named Iranistan, the house looked like a grand palace. The grounds had gardens, ponds, and fruit trees. The barns housed birds,

cows, pigs, and horses. People from the town of Bridgeport were allowed to wander the grounds and visit the gardens anytime they wanted.

Then Taylor heard about a Swedish singer named Jenny Lind. He thought she could be his next big star. Taylor wanted to bring Jenny to America.

Jenny Lind

Jenny was born in Stockholm, Sweden, in 1820, to a poor family. When she was nine, she attended the Royal Dramatic Theatre, where she studied music. By the time she was in her midtwenties, she had become the most famous singer in Europe. She sang for kings and queens. Composers wrote operas for her. Critics raved about her singing.

She was nicknamed "the Swedish Nightingale" for her clear, birdlike voice.

Everyone seemed to love Jenny. Offstage, she acted like any other ordinary girl. She treated common people the same as royalty. She was kind and donated most of the money from her performances to charities.

Taylor had never heard Jenny sing, but he didn't need to. Her reputation was enough for him. He knew he could make her a star in the United States.

Jenny hesitated but finally agreed to sign with Taylor—but she made sure she would be paid very, very well. Taylor had to borrow money to pay the amount she demanded in advance.

Now Taylor had to figure out how to make Americans who had never heard of Jenny want to see her. He sent reviews of Jenny's concerts in Europe to American newspapers. He made sure they printed the stories about Jenny's humble upbringing and her donations to charity. He sent them pictures of her, too. By the time Jenny Lind arrived in the United States on September 1, 1850, people all over the country had heard of her. Thousands greeted the arrival of her ship in New York City and cheered for her.

Lindomania (1850–1852)

Before the Swedish singer Jenny Lind came to the United States, most Americans didn't know much about famous people, beside the president and a few military heroes. The excitement surrounding Jenny's arrival sparked a craze the newspapers called Lindomania. Suddenly everyone wanted to own something connected to the famous Jenny Lind.

Stores sold Jenny Lind photographs, posters, sheet music, and face creams. There were Jenny Lind hats, dresses, and gloves; and, of course, there were Jenny Lind dolls. People seemed to want anything with her name or picture on it—even Jenny Lind sausages! P. T. Barnum was one of the first people to realize that there were many ways to make money once you became famous. And Lindomania helped create the modern idea of being a true celebrity.

Jenny performed in sixteen cities between September 1850 and June 1851. The tour was a big success, but Jenny asked to be released from her contract after only 93 performances (out of the 150 that they had originally planned). Taylor agreed. The tour had been exhausting. Travel on rough steamship voyages and long train trips had been difficult.

Jenny and Taylor had made a great deal of money together. Taylor himself earned over $500,000 from the tour. He had plenty of money, and he felt that he had perfected the art of making people famous. He was successful beyond his dreams.

CHAPTER 7
The Art of Losing Money

After finishing the tour with Jenny, Taylor was happy to return to his home in Connecticut, in the summer of 1851. He was busy writing his  autobiography. *The Life of P. T. Barnum, Written by Himself* was published in 1854 and quickly became a best seller in the United States and Britain. Just a year later, Taylor announced that he was bankrupt—he had no money left to pay any of his debts. People were shocked. He had made so much money with Jenny Lind and Tom Thumb! The American Museum was still doing well. His autobiography was a success. What had happened?

Over the years, Taylor had fallen in love with Bridgeport, the city near his home. He tried to help build it up. He bought land there and rented it out to new businesses. He helped pay for bridges, factories, shops, and a hotel. He ended up spending more money than he made.

Taylor also lent money to a troublesome cousin who gambled it away. Worse yet, that same cousin falsely signed Taylor's name to loan documents to borrow even more money. When the money wasn't repaid, some of the companies sued Taylor. The lawsuits dragged on for years.

Taylor's biggest mistake might have been investing in several clock factories. He had hoped they would move to Bridgeport, where they would provide jobs. However, the plan didn't quite work. Taylor lost over half a million dollars on one factory alone.

Taylor slowly worked his way out of bankruptcy. He begged the people who owed him money to pay him back. He gave up the luxury of smoking cigars. And he took on any job he could find managing tours and stage acts in Europe.

In 1858, friends in London suggested that Taylor do a lecture tour about all his business successes. It seemed like an odd choice of topic. Everyone knew he had lost so much money recently. But when he *was* successful, he had also made quite a lot. Taylor's lecture, titled "The Art of Money-Getting, or Success in Life," was a big hit. He was a fine speaker, and he included lots of jokes and stories in his lectures. The popular

speaking tour helped him earn money and recover from bankruptcy. Years later, Taylor published his notes from the tour as a book called *The Art of Money-Getting*.

Barnum's Golden Rules for Money-Getting

Here are ten of P. T. Barnum's golden rules:

- Choose a job you love and one that you are good at.
- Choose the right location for your business.
- Stay out of debt.
- Keep trying.
- Whatever you do, do it with all your might.
- Hire the best people you can find.
- Learn some useful skills.
- Focus on one business.
- Advertise!
- Be good to your customers.

CHAPTER 8
Joining the Circus

By 1861, the Civil War had begun in the
United States, and Taylor passionately supported
Abraham Lincoln and the Union side. When he
was younger, he had not given much thought to

the question of slavery. But by the time the war began, he had become a serious abolitionist—a person who believed that slavery in the United States needed to end. He produced pro-Union plays and spoke out against slavery in lectures at his American Museum.

The war convinced Taylor that he should enter politics. He wanted to continue to speak out against slavery. Taylor was elected to the Connecticut State General Assembly in April 1865 as a member of the Union (or Republican) Party.

The Civil War

The American Civil War began in April 1861. The Southern states, or the Confederates, wanted residents of new states to have the right to own slaves. Those in the Northern states—the Union— wanted to outlaw slavery altogether. President

Abraham Lincoln signed the Emancipation Proclamation in January 1863, declaring that all slaves "henceforth shall be free."

But the war turned into America's bloodiest conflict. When the Civil War finally ended in April 1865, the Union had been victorious, but over six hundred thousand men had lost their lives.

In July, Taylor was giving a speech to the state assembly when he received terrible news: The American Museum had burned down. A fire had started in a furnace in the basement. The museum was destroyed in less than an hour.

Taylor immediately went to work rebuilding the museum. He found another building just a mile north of the old location and collected new items to exhibit. Just two months later, the second American Museum opened.

Taylor fought in the state assembly to change Connecticut laws so African Americans could vote. But the law didn't pass. He ran for the US Congress in 1867. But he lost to his own distant relative named William Barnum.

Taylor decided to buy a town house in New York City. He could easily attend to his business there and visit his daughters, who were all married and living in the city by then. He and Charity also had another house in Bridgeport, near the Connecticut seashore. Charity wasn't well, and doctors suggested that the sea air might make her feel better.

In 1868, the second American Museum burned down! This time Taylor didn't want to rebuild.

He was fifty-eight years old. He wondered if he should simply retire.

Then in late 1870, Taylor got an offer he could not resist. William C. Coup and Dan Castello, two circus managers, ran a show called the Egyptian Caravan. They wanted Taylor to partner with them to create a new show. Taylor had been bored, and he missed the excitement of show business. He quickly agreed.

The new circus had performers, a collection of live animals, and an exhibition of interesting objects, like wax figures, mechanical toys, and a mummy. Coup and Castello managed the day-to-day matters of the circus. Taylor contributed his famous name and genius for publicity.

William C. Coup — Dan Castello

Taylor had flyers printed with stories and pictures about all the different acts in the show, now called P. T. Barnum's Great Traveling Museum, Menagerie, Caravan, and Hippodrome. They were sent ahead of the circus to each upcoming city and distributed throughout the nearby towns. By the time the circus arrived, the townspeople knew all about the show and were anxious to see it.

The new show started its first tour in April 1871. When audiences arrived, they walked through the menagerie of animals and the sideshow of museum curiosities. Then they entered the big tent to watch the performers: acrobats, clowns, musicians, and animal trainers.

It was a huge success. Although the circus tents could hold thousands of people, the shows regularly sold out. The *shape* of the show was part of the problem.

Years earlier, circuses

had started out as shows featuring daredevil horseback riders who rode in a circle around a ring-shaped arena. The circular shape became standard even as other performers were added. As circuses became more popular, their owners added more rows of seats. But more rows meant people sat farther away from the show. They couldn't see what was happening in the ring. Taylor solved this problem by adding a second ring—another circular arena—under the big tent. This allowed more people to sit under the tent. Everyone could see the performances in both rings.

Taylor was now sixty-two years old. But he was still working hard to promote the circus and dream up new ideas to make it even better. He added a new line to the 1872 show's posters: "The Greatest Show on Earth." The phrase caught on, and soon that was what everyone called P. T. Barnum's circus. Then he had an idea that would change circuses forever. Why not move the show by train instead of horse and wagon?

Taylor's circus train could be loaded and unloaded quickly. It could travel up to a hundred miles overnight, much farther than the old horse

and wagons. The performers could also sleep better than they could on bumpy wagons. By the time they arrived in the next town in the morning, everyone was ready for a full day of performing.

In 1873, Taylor traveled to Europe on business. While he was in Germany, he received news that Charity had died. Taylor was very sad. He remained in his room alone for several days. He and Charity had been married for forty-four years. When he emerged, Taylor was ready to continue with the business of running the Greatest Show on Earth.

The Circus Train

In 1872, the first circus-owned train was made up of sixty-five cars. The circus train carried everything the Greatest Show on Earth required, including circus wagons, tents, poles, animals, food, supplies, and living quarters for all the performers, the animal trainers, and the circus crew.

Eventually, the Ringling Brothers and Barnum & Bailey Circus traveled by two different circus trains: a blue line and a red line that alternated yearly schedules.

CHAPTER 9
Jumbo

Taylor surprised everyone by marrying again in September 1874. He was sixty-four years old. His new wife was twenty-four-year-old Nancy Fish, the daughter of John Fish, one of Taylor's friends.

Taylor and Nancy moved into a new seaside house in Connecticut. Taylor's daughters all had children by this time, and Taylor entertained his grandchildren with pony rides, pranks, and magic tricks—just as his own fun-loving grandfather had for him.

Taylor cared deeply about Connecticut, and especially the town of Bridgeport. When he was asked to run for mayor of the city in 1875, he gladly agreed. He won easily, and then was elected mayor again in 1877. He went on to be elected a representative to the state General Assembly, and even ran for the US Senate in 1880 but lost.

That was okay with Taylor, though. He was proud to serve his state, but he was a showman at heart. He was still busy with his circus.

Later that year, Taylor decided to end his partnership with Coup and Castello. He had received an offer to work with James A. Bailey, another very successful circus manager, and he thought they could put on an even bigger show together. When the circus went back on the road

 in the spring of 1881, it had a new addition—a third ring to make room for more acts and bigger audiences. Just a year later, Taylor made the biggest addition to his circus yet: Jumbo the elephant.

Jumbo was born in East Africa, in or around 1860. He was the first known African elephant to be brought to Europe. He had been a popular

part of the Regent's Park Zoo in London since 1865. Jumbo was eleven feet tall and weighed six tons, making him the largest elephant in captivity. Thousands of people a year came to see Jumbo at the zoo, feed him treats, and ride him.

Taylor had always been fond of elephants and had wished he could bring Jumbo to the United States to join his circus. In 1882, he offered the Regent's Park Zoo $10,000 for Jumbo. He never thought the zoo would sell him, though. To everyone's surprise, the zoo accepted Taylor's offer.

Londoners were very sad that their beloved Jumbo was being taken away. Newspapers printed angry articles about the sale of Jumbo. Thousands of children wrote letters to the zoo, to Jumbo, and to Taylor. The London Zoological Society went to court to try to stop the sale but failed.

Taylor thought this was great publicity. He made sure everyone in America knew how upset the British were about losing Jumbo. It helped stir up interest in the new circus star. He wanted to let Americans know that they would be lucky to have a chance to see Jumbo in person.

When it was time for Jumbo to walk from the zoo to the ship that would carry him to America, Jumbo laid down in a London street and refused to move. The British saw this as evidence that

Jumbo didn't want to leave them. Taylor said to let him stay there as long as he wanted. It was free advertising! Eventually Jumbo boarded the ship to New York.

Americans were already in the grip of "Jumbomania" by the time the huge elephant arrived in April 1882.

Jumbo was the star of the circus for the next few years. Many people came to the show just to see the six-ton elephant. But on September 15,

1885, tragedy struck. The circus was in Ontario, Canada. After the last show of the night, the animals were being led onto their train cars when an unexpected train came rushing down the tracks and hit Jumbo. The force of the crash was so great that it knocked the train right off the tracks. The famous elephant died within minutes.

People all over the world were deeply saddened by Jumbo's death. But Taylor had an idea that would give people one more chance to see Jumbo.

Jumbomania (1882–1885)

The Jumbomania craze started before Jumbo even got to America. The largest elephant in captivity commanded a lot of attention and had plenty of fans. People wanted to buy anything with Jumbo's name or picture on it, even if they hadn't seen him in person as part of P. T. Barnum's Greatest Show on Earth.

Souvenirs of Jumbo included pictures, hats, neckties, bracelets, fans, and earrings. People eagerly bought Jumbo soap, cigars, stoves, thread, and baking powder. There were even songs and poems written about Jumbo.

Taylor had the huge African elephant stuffed. He preserved the skeleton separately. Stuffed Jumbo went on tour with the circus alongside his own skeleton. The "Double Jumbo" exhibit was very popular. When the tour was finished, Jumbo's skeleton was sent to the American Museum of Natural History in New York. The stuffed Jumbo

was sent to Tufts University in Massachusetts, where Taylor had donated money to build the Barnum Museum of Natural History (now called Barnum Hall).

Taylor had made Jumbo into a big star. And Jumbo had helped make the circus a lasting success.

CHAPTER 10
The End of the Show

In 1888, Taylor briefly considered running for president. But he didn't have quite enough support within his political party and he was not nominated. Taylor decided that he was finally done with politics.

The next year, Taylor and Nancy moved into a new home. He was nearly eighty, but he was working on making yet another of his dreams come true. He wanted to bring the Greatest Show on Earth to England.

It took time, money, and a lot of planning to figure out how to get the whole show—the performers, animals, and crew—onto ships. But it was worth the effort. The three-ring circus was a big hit in London.

Barnum & Bailey circus parade, England

Taylor had a great time. By then he was a well-known figure in England, and he enjoyed meeting old friends, making new ones, and telling stories about his adventures.

In 1890, Taylor published a book called *Funny Stories Told by Phineas T. Barnum*. He had never stopped writing. Each year he had published an additional chapter to his autobiography so it was always up-to-date. He made Nancy promise that when he died, she would publish a final chapter that would include his last days and end the story.

The autobiography was one way for Taylor to make sure he got a chance to tell his story *his* way. When his business partners wanted to make a big statue of Taylor, he agreed on one condition: that the statue not be revealed while he was alive. Taylor loved the finished statue. Then he ordered it put away in a warehouse.

Taylor had had a stroke in November 1890 and never fully recovered. He spent his last months at his seaside home, watching the ocean along the Connecticut coast and greeting the many visitors who came to see him. He happily gave interviews

to reporters. Phineas Taylor Barnum died on April 7, 1891. He was buried in his beloved town of Bridgeport. The statue that had been made years before was brought out of the warehouse. It was put in Seaside Park, a Bridgeport park that Taylor had helped build.

Taylor was successful because he knew how to get people excited and interested in new ideas, whether a fake mermaid or an unknown Swedish singer.  He believed that you could never advertise too much, and he believed in putting on a good show.

Advertisers today still use Taylor's ideas. Movie studios always release trailers for new movies months before the movies open in the same way Taylor built up excitement months before Jenny Lind came to the United States. He also did this when he planted letters in the newspapers to introduce people to the Fejee Mermaid. Today he might have been the king of viral videos and a master of Twitter. His legendary showmanship remains unrivaled.

The Last Show

Barnum & Bailey's Greatest Show on Earth, as it was known in 1891, continued under James Bailey's management until 1906.

The Ringling Brothers circus bought the Barnum & Bailey Circus and ran it separately until 1919, when it became known as the Ringling Brothers and Barnum & Bailey Circus.

In 1957, a promoter named Irvin Feld oversaw the move from performing in tents to performing in large arenas. Feld Entertainment bought the Ringling Brothers and Barnum & Bailey Circus in 1967.

Under growing pressure from animal rights groups, the circus announced that it would be elephant-free by 2016.

But the cost of running the show and declining ticket sales made it impossible to keep going. The last show was on May 21, 2017.

Phineas Taylor Barnum loved his audiences and loved entertaining people. His shows, museums, books, and circus brought new ideas, scientific curiosities, and a whole lot of fun to millions of people during his lifetime. The little boy who loved his grandfather's practical jokes became one of the world's greatest entertainers.

In December 2017, a movie called *The Greatest Showman* was released. It starred Hugh Jackman as P. T. Barnum and became one of the surprise hits of the year.

Timeline of P. T. Barnum's Life

1810 — Born on July 5

1826 — Begins to work as a store clerk

1829 — Marries Charity Hallett

1835 — Begins to exhibit Joice Heth, supposed 161-year-old woman

1841 — Buys American Museum

1842 — Discovers and exhibits Fejee Mermaid and Tom Thumb

1850 — Begins touring with the singer Jenny Lind

1854 — Publishes best-selling autobiography

1865 — First elected to Connecticut State General Assembly

1870 — Partners with William C. Coup and Dan Castello to manage a circus

1871 — P. T. Barnum's Great Traveling Museum, Menagerie, Caravan, and Hippodrome opens

1872 — Adds "The Greatest Show on Earth" to circus name

1873 — Wife Charity dies

1874 — Marries Nancy Fish

1875 — Elected mayor of Bridgeport

1880 — Starts new partnership with circus manager James A. Bailey

1882 — Buys Jumbo the elephant from the London Zoo

1891 — Dies on April 7

Timeline of the World

1809	Abraham Lincoln is born
1813	Jane Austen's *Pride and Prejudice* is published
1815	Napoleon is defeated at the Battle of Waterloo
1823	Thomas Young and Jean-François Champollion decipher the Rosetta Stone
1829	The first braille book for blind readers is published
1836	Santa Anna's Mexican army defeats the Texans at the Alamo
1840	The first postage stamp is introduced in Britain
1846	The first official baseball game is played
1848	Gold is discovered in California
1859	John Brown leads the antislavery raid on Harper's Ferry
1861	The Civil War begins
1865	The Civil War ends
	Abraham Lincoln is assassinated
1871	The Great Chicago Fire burns down the city
1872	Yellowstone National Park becomes the world's first national park
1881	The American Red Cross is established
1886	An Atlanta pharmacist creates Coca-Cola
1889	The Eiffel Tower opens
1891	Dr. James Naismith invents the game of basketball

Bibliography

Barnum, P. T. *The Life of P. T. Barnum, Written by Himself.* New York: Redfield, 1855.

Cook, James W. (ed.). *The Colossal P. T. Barnum Reader: Nothing Else Like It in the Universe.* Urbana, IL: University of Illinois Press, 2005.

Harris, Neil. *Humbug: The Art of P. T. Barnum.* Chicago: The University of Chicago Press, 1981. First published 1973 by Little, Brown.

Saxon, A. H. *P. T. Barnum: The Legend and the Man.* New York: Columbia University Press, 1989.